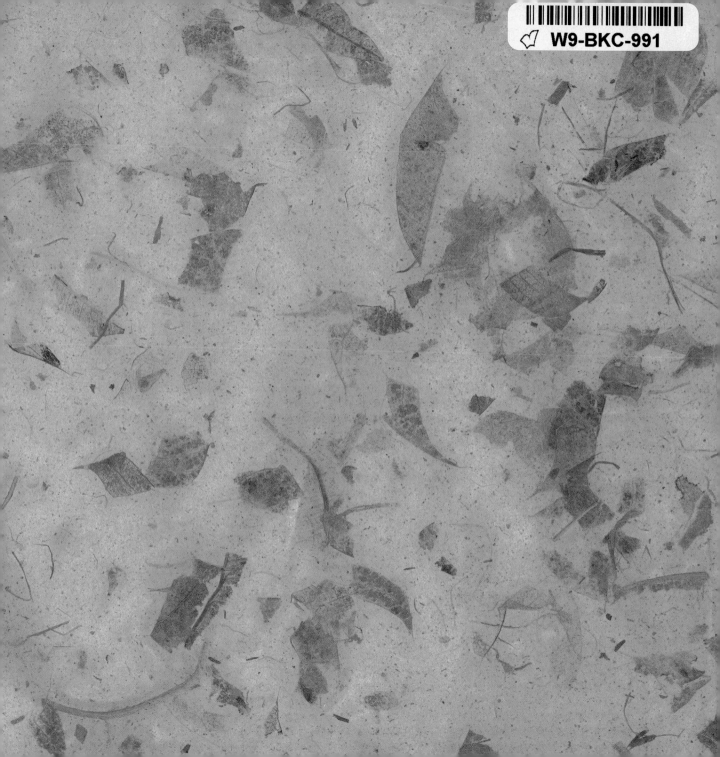

W9-BKC-991

LOOK FOR THESE OTHER BOOKS ABOUT OUR HOLIDAYS:

THE STORY OF CHRISTMAS

THE STORY OF EASTER

THE STORY OF HANUKKAH

THE STORY OF KWANZAA

THE STORY OF PASSOVER

THE STORY OF SHABBAT

The Story of Thanksgiving

by Robert Merrill Bartlett

illustrated by Sally Wern Comport

HarperCollins*Publishers*

INDIANAPOLIS MARION CO PUBLIC LIBRARY

For Sarah Elizabeth
—R.M.B.

To my family, with a heart full of thanksgiving for your spirit
—S.W.C.

The publisher gratefully acknowledges both Heather Henson and
Susan Bartlett Weber for their invaluable assistance.

The publisher and author would like to thank Jennifer Tolpa of the
Massachusetts Historical Society for her time and expert review.

The text for this book was first published in *Thanksgiving Day*, a Crowell Holiday Book edited by Susan Bartlett Weber,
written by Robert Merrill Bartlett and illustrated by W. T. Mars, in 1965.
The Story of Thanksgiving Text copyright © 2001 by the Estate of Robert Merrill Bartlett
Illustrations copyright © 2001 by Sally Wern Comport
Printed in the U.S.A. All rights reserved. www.harperchildrens.com

Library of Congress Cataloging-in-Publication Data
Bartlett, Robert Merrill.
    The story of Thanksgiving / by Robert Merrill Bartlett ; illustrated by Sally Wern Comport.
        p.   cm.
    Rev. ed.: Thanksgiving Day. c1965.
    Summary: Relates the history and customs of Thanksgiving, from the harvest festivals of the ancient world and the first
Thanksgiving in colonial America to today's celebrations.
    ISBN 0-06-028778-0. — ISBN 0-06-028779-9 (lib. bdg.)
    1. Thanksgiving Day—Juvenile literature.   [1. Thanksgiving Day.   2. Pilgrims (New Plymouth Colony)   3. Holidays.]
I. Comport, Sally Wern, ill.   II. Bartlett, Robert Merrill. Thanksgiving Day.   III. Title.
GT4975.B39   2001   99-41337
394.2649—dc21   CIP

Typography by Al Cetta   1   2   3   4   5   6   7   8   9   10   ❖   Revised and Newly Illustrated Edition

The Story
of
Thanksgiving

eople have always given thanks at harvesttime. They are glad to have food for the winter and celebrate with feasting and prayers of thanksgiving. On the fourth Thursday of November, Americans gather with friends and family to give thanks for their blessings and feast on delicious food.

Our Thanksgiving is a mix of several traditions. One tradition goes back to the Pilgrims, who shared a huge feast with their Wampanoag friends and who thanked God for their good life after a year of hardship in a new land. But giving thanks also goes back to harvest festivals held by many different people all over the world.

Long ago the people of Greece had a harvest festival. It was in the fall, after the grain was cut. Ripe apples, pears, and plums hung on the trees.

Heralds traveled from village to village. They blew their trumpets and called everyone to the celebration. The people visited shrines of Demeter, the goddess of the harvest. They carried gifts of grain to lay before her.

The Romans too gave thanks at harvest season. Their goddess was Ceres. They believed Ceres guarded their crops and made them grow well. The Romans honored her with parades, dancing, sports, and feasting.

Another ancient thanksgiving was the Feast of Booths. It was celebrated by the Jews. They were called Hebrews then and lived in the land of Canaan.

At harvesttime the Hebrews built little booths from branches and leaves. In them they placed fruits and vegetables from the fields. Then they gave thanks to God for their crops.

ater the Christians in Europe said prayers to bless the planting and reaping of the harvest. They believed that God watched over the seeds in the earth.

At harvesttime the farmers decorated themselves with ribbons and flowers. They sang as they walked home beside their wagons full of grain.

When European explorers and settlers came to the New World, they brought many of their customs with them. In 1621 the Pilgrims became the first group of English colonists to hold a harvest celebration on American soil. Today we think of this celebration as the first Thanksgiving.

The Pilgrims were English citizens who came to America in search of a new home. Half of the group were Puritans, who demanded the right to read the Bible and worship God as they chose. In England the Puritans were often thrown in prison and even killed for their beliefs. Some fled to Holland, where they lived for twelve years. But they wanted a country of their own. So they planned to sail to the English colonies in America.

The Puritans joined with others who wanted to live in the New World. The Puritans called these people "Strangers." But later they would all be known as Pilgrims.

In September 1620, one hundred and two men, women, and children set sail on a little ship called the *Mayflower*. They cooked, ate, and slept all crowded together. The stormy voyage lasted sixty-five days, and the passengers were often very seasick. Finally, on November 21, the *Mayflower* reached Cape Cod.

For several weeks the Pilgrims explored Cape Cod. Then they sailed across Massachusetts Bay to Plymouth. There they found a safe harbor and springs of fresh water. They began to build houses right away, so they would have shelter for the winter ahead.

No one was living in Plymouth then. A sickness had killed many of the Wampanoag people who had lived there, and the rest had moved away.

That winter the Pilgrims had very little food to eat. They were always hungry and cold. Nearly all of them became sick, and half of them died.

When spring came, two men named Squanto and Samoset appeared and made friends with the surviving Pilgrims.

Squanto lived with the Wampanoag tribe, who had been in the region for generations. Squanto could speak English. He had been kidnapped by English traders who wanted to sell him as a slave in Spain. But he escaped and got away to England. There a sea captain brought him back home.

Samoset could also speak a little English. Later Samoset brought Massasoit to visit. Massasoit was Great Sachem, or chief of the Wampanoags. The Pilgrims and Massasoit made a treaty of peace. For fifty-five years there was no fighting between the English and the Wampanoags.

The Wampanoags gave the Pilgrims corn, beans, and squash to plant that first spring. They showed them how to catch herring, eels, and lobsters and where to dig for clams.

The Pilgrims stood guard over the fields with their muskets to keep crows from eating the seeds. They watched until the first green blades peeked through the soil. They knew their lives depended on this harvest.

In the fall the Pilgrims gathered the crops. The wheat and barley had grown well. The corn that the Wampanoags had taught them to plant had grown best of all.

The Pilgrims wanted to celebrate their harvest. In October of 1621 they held their first thanksgiving. They invited the Wampanoags to join them.

Like the Pilgrims, the Wampanoags had a tradition of celebrating at harvesttime. Chief Massasoit brought ninety men with him to Plymouth. They gave the Pilgrims five deer for roasting.

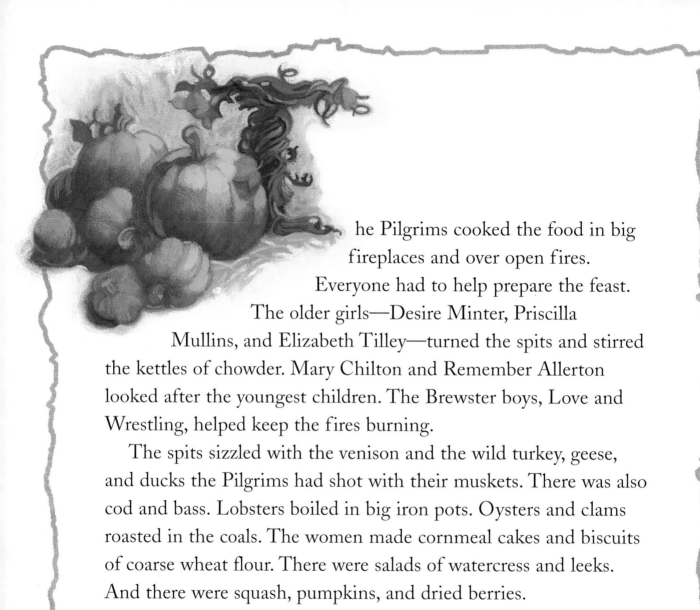

he Pilgrims cooked the food in big fireplaces and over open fires.

Everyone had to help prepare the feast. The older girls—Desire Minter, Priscilla Mullins, and Elizabeth Tilley—turned the spits and stirred the kettles of chowder. Mary Chilton and Remember Allerton looked after the youngest children. The Brewster boys, Love and Wrestling, helped keep the fires burning.

The spits sizzled with the venison and the wild turkey, geese, and ducks the Pilgrims had shot with their muskets. There was also cod and bass. Lobsters boiled in big iron pots. Oysters and clams roasted in the coals. The women made cornmeal cakes and biscuits of coarse wheat flour. There were salads of watercress and leeks. And there were squash, pumpkins, and dried berries.

At last the food was ready. People ate with their fingers or with clamshells. There were some spoons and knives, but no forks. The plates were made of wood or pewter. There was wine made from wild grapes and beer made from barley.

The Pilgrims wore bright clothes of green, red, blue, purple, and russet brown. The Wampanoags wore aprons of deer leather. They had skins of fox, bear, or moose about their shoulders. Some had feathers in their well-greased hair. Their faces were painted with red and white lines.

The Pilgrims did not consider this day a holy one. If they had, there would not have been a feast. There would have been fasting and prayer. But since this was meant to be a harvest celebration, it was a festive and noisy party.

After the feasting everyone played games and had contests. There were footraces and wrestling and pitching the bar. The Wampanoags shot their bows and arrows. The Pilgrims marched and fired their muskets.

After three days the Wampanoags went home and the Pilgrims went back to their daily chores. They looked in the woods for nuts and hunted and fished for food. They sawed logs, traded for furs, and picked sassafras, which they sent to England to help pay for the *Mayflower* voyage.

Neither the Pilgrims nor the Wampanoags knew that they had started Thanksgiving. There were no plans to have another harvest celebration—unless the crops were successful again the next year.

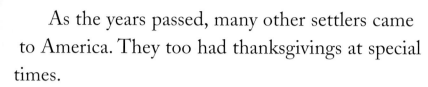

As the years passed, many other settlers came to America. They too had thanksgivings at special times.

In Puritan communities the celebration became a more solemn one. After the crops were in, the town leaders would proclaim a day of fasting. People put on their best clothes and went to church.

There they said prayers and sang hymns. Other colonists had a family thanks-giving more like we do today—with loved ones gathered around a special meal.

Sometimes there was dancing or parades, just as in Roman times. Children played games just as the Pilgrims had done.

Whether solemn or festive, these early American thanksgivings were always held in the fall after a good harvest. But there was no special date set aside for the holiday, and it was not celebrated regularly each year.

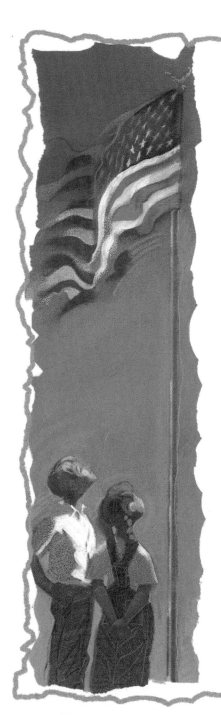

In 1789 George Washington, the first president of the United States, proclaimed a day of thanksgiving for all Americans. People everywhere gave thanks for winning their freedom from England in the American Revolution.

But still, Americans did not have a thanksgiving every year. It did not become an annual holiday until 1863. By then the country was divided by the Civil War, when North and South fought each other over the question of slavery. President Lincoln declared that the last Thursday of November would be Thanksgiving Day. He hoped the holiday would bring a spirit of unity to a nation broken in two.

Today Thanksgiving is a happy time when families gather together. People give thanks for the good things in their lives, just like the Puritans who rejoiced for their blessings, and like the farmers in Europe who sang beside their wagons full of grain.

Then comes the feast. Grandparents, parents, brothers and sisters, uncles, aunts, cousins, and friends meet around a long dinner table. The roast turkey is carved. There is stuffing and potatoes, yams and squash, cranberries, and finally, pumpkin pie. They eat and eat. And talk and talk. Perhaps they are just as noisy as the Pilgrims and the Wampanoags were at that first American Thanksgiving.

Things to Do and Make at Thanksgiving

"Over the River and Through the Woods" was a favorite song to sing after a Thanksgiving feast in the late 1800s.

O- ver the ri- ver and through the woods, to Grand-moth-er's house we
O- ver the ri- ver and through the woods, trot fast my dap- ple

go. The horse knows the way to car- ry the sleigh through the
gray! Spring o- ver the ground like a hunt- ing hound for

white and drift- ed snow—. O- ver the ri- ver and
this is Thanks-giv- ing Day —! O- ver the ri- ver and

through the woods, Oh, how the wind does blow! It
through the woods, Now Grand-moth-er's cap I spy! Hur-

stings the toes and bites the nose as o- ver the fields we go.
rah for the fun! Is the pudding done? Hur- rah for the pumpkin pie!

Pumpkin Muffins

(MAKES 12 MUFFINS)

At Thanksgiving it's fun to eat foods, like pumpkins and cranberries, that are native to North and South America. Ask an adult to help you make these delicious Thanksgiving treats.

Preheat the oven to 400 degrees.
Grease muffin tins or use paper muffin cups inside tins.

INGREDIENTS:

1½ cups flour	¼ cup shortening
½ cup sugar	1 egg (beaten)
2 teaspoons baking powder	½ cup unsweetened canned pumpkin
¾ teaspoon salt	½ cup milk
½ teaspoon cinnamon	½ cup raisins
½ teaspoon nutmeg	

Mix flour, sugar, baking powder, salt, and spices. In a separate bowl, combine shortening, egg (already beaten), pumpkin, and milk. Add to the dry mixture and mix until just moistened. Stir in raisins. Fill greased muffin tins or paper muffin cups two-thirds full. Sprinkle a pinch of sugar over each muffin. Bake for 18 to 20 minutes, until a knife inserted into the center of one muffin comes out clean.

9/11 14 11/10
11/12-17
1/13

7
11-05

2-02

Indianapolis
Marion County
Public Library

Withdrawn

Renew by Phone
269-5222

Renew on the Web
www.imcpl.org

For general Library information
please call 269-1700.